MW00439095

When Parents Are at War

A Child Therapist's Guide To Navigating High Conflict Divorce & Custody Cases

Lynn Louise Wonders

Copyright©2019 Lynn Louise Wonders. All rights reserved.
Published and Printed in the United States of America
Second Edition

For information about permission to reproduce selections from this publication please contact Wonders Counseling Services, LLC at www. WondersCounseling.com

Disclaimer and Important Note to Readers

The content in this publication does not represent legal advice and should not replace legal advice from an attorney at law. It is my strong recommendation that you retain an attorney licensed and practicing in your state or province for yourself and your therapy practice with whom you can consult on any and all legal questions and represent you if and when needed. The guidance and recommendations in this publication are reflective of some of my own experiences and are strictly for the purpose of general clinical case conceptualization, treatment planning and self-care for mental health professionals working with children and families in clinical private practice settings. The content in this publication does not substitute for clinical supervision, appropriate training, or peer review and consultation. It is my strong recommendation that you consult with a seasoned, licensed mental health supervisor for case supervision and consultation when you have high conflict divorce and custody related cases. The publisher and author of this publication cannot guarantee the complete accuracy, efficacy, or appropriateness of any recommendations herein. Any references to past or current clinical cases are in the context of general conceptualization and are not specific to any particular client or case. No identifying client information is referenced or revealed in this publication and any perceived recognition of identifying information is purely coincidence as many high conflict divorce and custody cases share similar circumstances.

ISBN: 9781797802893

Dedication

I dedicate this book to all of the brave and dedicated therapists I have had the honor of supervising and guiding on the journey of helping children and families; my own three children Jonathan, Patrick and Madeline who have patiently endured their mom's long hours of work over the years; my own supervisors and mentors; all of the fair-minded, child-focused attorneys and guardians ad litem whom I've had the honor of working with over the years; and to my husband Dennis, who has been my grounding force and personal support through some very challenging times in the course of my career.

Acknowledgments

I want to acknowledge all of the therapists I have supervised and consulted with on tough clinical cases throughout the United States, in Israel, Australia, Ireland, England and South Korea, and all of the therapists in my online community *Growing a Play Therapy Practice.* This book has developed because many of you have asked me to collect all of my guidance in one place for easy reference. Thank you for your encouragement and for the steadfast dedication you have shown to your own work with children and families and to the worldwide community we share online.

I want to mention a few of my many wonderful colleagues. Jen Taylor, LCSW, RPT-S, a fellow pioneer spirit in the field of play therapy and online learning has been an inspiration and a great encourager. Thank you for helping me bring my distance play therapy training to therapists all over the world. Liz Gray, LCSW, RPT, your stead-fast support with your organizational expertise, your help with my blogging and webinar production, managing the online community and your help proof reading and editing the manuscript for this book. Kate Fagan, Nelson, LCSW and Courtney McVey, LCSW I am so thankful to both of you for your help with the process of proof-reading and editing my manuscript. Jamie Lynn Langley, LCSW, RPT-S, Lauren Gasper, LCSW, RPT and Erin Moncure, LPC, RPT I so appreciate your generous endorsements of this book.

My sons Jonathan and Patrick, you were so very young when I began this career path and now are happy, healthy, successful grown men. Raising you and attending to your healthy development all the way into adulthood has been a tremendous motivator for my learning and my career development. Without your patience and love I would never have been able to do the things I've done in my career to make this book possible. Madeline, you have experienced and witnessed so much in your own life and your resilience and ability to see the good in everyone balanced with an uncanny sense of realism has been a tremendous inspiration to me. I love you, all three.

I've worked with some amazing attorneys, custody evaluators and guardians ad litem over the years and I want to acknowledge the excellent professionals in the metro Atlanta, Georgia area with whom I've worked on the toughest of cases. Your dedication to the best interest of the children in these high conflict cases is so appreciated. Thank you for your professionalism and for the good work you do. I've learned a lot from you along the way.

And finally, I want to acknowledge and thank my husband LCDR Dennis Wonders, who served our country in the US Navy for 20 years, served the public school system founding and directing a stellar, nationally recognized JROTC program and who has been by my side throughout my career as a therapist, seeing first-hand how the nature of my work with high conflict divorce and custody cases can take its toll. Thank you for keeping me grounded and helping me to return to dedicated practices of self-care when I temporarily lost sight. We've experienced a lot together on a personal level that has influenced my dedication to helping children and families and your love and loyalty to me and our three children has been a profound source of support.

Contents

Contents

What You Need to Know
and Why You Need to Know it

IF YOU ARE a therapist who works with children and families, this book is for you.

Whether you are fearless when it comes to accepting new child clients who have parents going through a divorce or whether you are anxious and avoidant of these cases, this book is for you.

Whether you think you already know what you need to do with cases that put you at risk of involvement with family court litigation or if you feel completely unequipped and unprepared, this book is for you.

My first job after college was working in a busy law firm as a paralegal in which I had front row seats to observe the legal battles between parents going through divorce and custody disputes. I accompanied attorneys to court for hearings and trials many times, and most often I was the liaison who communicated with the anxious or irate clients who had retained the law firm to represent them. It was a high stress job. As the client-liaison, I quickly realized the emotional intensity and often challenging personalities of the people bent on fighting in court. I left to accept a position in higher education which later led to educational consulting with adolescents and their parents. I went on to complete a masters degree in professional counseling and psychology. I decided to specialize in working with children and families and I trained extensively to provide play therapy services. In serving this population, I found myself back in the midst of high conflict between parents going through divorce.

I obtained special training to serve as a *Child Specialist* within a legal process called *collaborative family law*. My role was to work with parents who were moving through a divorce without litigation but needed help with the development of their parenting plan. This plan was designed to serve the best interest of the children and the whole family, while the attorneys and financial professionals did their jobs to help parents move through the divorce process peacefully. While a wonderful concept, it's a model that is not often utilized. My theory says the reason it's a model that is rarely utilized is because the parents who are capable of collaboration usually go through the less expensive process of mediation; the parents who most need a team of professionals to help them collaborate are typically the ones wired for battle and headed for litigation.

During my career providing therapy for children and families, along with my years providing clinical supervision and consultation for therapists, I have experienced and witnessed the special challenges of working with families that were experiencing divorce or custody related conflict. Often, I observed parents so embroiled in their own battle with one another, they are incapable of seeing or hearing what is best for the children.

I'd be willing to bet that every therapist who sees child clients will eventually come in contact with cases in which the parents are at war with one another. It is important that all therapists who see children and families know how to establish and follow effective policies, protocols and professional boundaries in order to protect the integrity of the therapeutic process and ensure the self-care and wellbeing of the therapist.

I have been subpoenaed to court as an expert witness on numerous cases over the years. I have testified in many high conflict divorce and custody cases. I've worked with scores of guardians ad litem and attorneys since 2004. I have served as the court-ordered therapist by particular family court judges on many custody cases.

There was a time in my career when I had several cases at the same time in which I had been appointed by the court to provide therapy for children and families involved in high conflict divorce and custody disputes. I saw extreme cases of alienated children and levels of high conflict between parents at that time. These particular cases were all very intense and draining. Believing at the time I could handle those extreme high conflict cases simultaneously was a mistake from which I learned some important lessons.

Even with implementation of all of the protocols I share with you in this book, my own wellbeing was negatively impacted because these kinds of cases simply demand an inordinate amount of time and energy. I was working very long and late hours. I was spending hours in consultation with guardians ad litem and several days in court every month providing testimony. I was having to change and adapt treatment plans more often than normal due to the complex dynamics and circumstances of these cases. I was faced with threatening, pathological behavior from parents. My sleep was disrupted with intrusive images and thoughts along with excessive worry for the children in these families.

Once all of those cases finally came to a close, I paused on accepting new clients in order to create time and space for intense self-care and reevaluation of what it takes to serve the needs of these kinds of families without burning out. I began writing about these experiences. There is truly something powerful about thoughtful hindsight. I decided to take these experiences and create something helpful for child therapists so that I might help others avoid the often unforeseen hazards of working with high conflict cases. I offered an online training seminar that has since been taken by hundreds of therapists all over the country. I began leading self-care retreats for therapists, started an online community and taught ethics courses focused on self-care for therapists. I often lead supervision groups that focus on high conflict divorce and custody cases, and I've conducted hundreds of high conflict case consultation sessions with therapists all over the United States. There is a need for this information to get into more hands of more therapists.

The bottom line is that high conflict divorce and custody cases are complex, very challenging, and can be exhausting and emotionally draining for therapists. I am on a mission to help therapists avoid the pitfalls that often come along with these kinds of cases.

I have seen over time that there is a continuum of intensity and severity to consider. You are likely to discover that following the policies and protocols suggested in this book will help you to successfully corral and redirect parents who are exhibiting signs of high conflict. You may find that you are able to implement particular policies so you can do your job in helping the child and family in therapy.

Occasionally you will find the level of conflict between parents is so high that the agenda of one or both parents has little or nothing to do with the child receiving help and support from you. With these cases you may find yourself feeling like a pawn in their war-game, often fueled by litigation attorneys who are understandably focused on doing a job they've been hired to do.

It's important for therapists to understand that family law attorneys are hired to represent their clients in order to get the best outcome for those clients. One family attorney I worked with years ago explained to me that the job he is hired to do involves "fighting to win."

As therapists, we are paid to help people heal, grow and develop skills for healthy, productive communication and harmony within relationships. Divorce attorneys are typically hired to go to battle in court on behalf of their clients, if needed. While attorneys on each side are very often able to help the clients reach a settlement outside of court, most family lawyers are prepared to fight as needed to win the case. While we may share the same client with an attorney, what we are doing as therapist for the client can feel contrary to what the attorney's aim is.

Over the years, my observation is that the lawyer's brain simply works differently than a therapist's brain. The training received in law school along with law firm experience is quite different than the training we receive in graduate school and in our own clinical field-work. As a therapist, your first line of thinking is consideration for the best interest of a child's mental, physical and emotional well-being in the context of the family system. Your aim is to provide strengthening, healing, harmonizing and resolution of conflict. The family law attorney is hired to represent one side of a divorce and custody case, and therefore, is focused on winning the case for that client. In order to win the case, the attorney will sometimes work to paint a bad picture of the other parent for the court. While our aim as therapists is to help a family see each other with understanding and work together positively, the aim of the lawyer is to win the case or at least get the best outcome possible for the client.

I have worked with a number of very equanimous attorneys who are willing and capable of focusing on the best interest of the child caught in the middle of the parents' war. I can only imagine, however, that it is a difficult mind-set for an attorney to maintain when the family court system can be such a breeding ground for conflict. The very nature of divorce and custody litigation is set up for what I see as *polite combat*. There are always two sides with two opposing agendas. A courtroom is set up with a table on one side for the plaintiff and a table on the opposite side for the defendant. One parent vs. the other parent. There are legal documents filed with the court including a *complaint* along with *interrogatories*. The court is asked to hear *arguments* and issue *judgment* and *awards*.

Consider all this terminology and you can see that the court system is set up for battle. While the system is at times a necessary and helpful means for providing firm rules that parents are legally bound to follow, much of the time the family court system can feed an already existing high conflict dynamic. When you mix in all of the intense emotions typically felt and expressed by parents when there is dissolution of marriage and division of a family, you can imagine how easy it is for the whole thing to go off the rails.

It is not my intention to engender fear. I hope to help you develop greater *awareness* of what you need to know in order to be empowered and prepared so that you will know when to refer out the cases that are beyond your scope of training. I also want you to be prepared for how to develop and observe a plan for handling potentially hazardous clinical circumstances *before* you find yourself sinking in what feels like an impossible situation.

These very high conflict cases are not the norm overall. It is common, however, for these cases to find their way to the therapy office. Often an attorney representing a parent in a custody dispute recommends that the child see a therapist as part of the legal strategy, setting you up as a potential witness. I'd like to see fewer therapists stepping into these cases unwittingly and unprepared.

All too often, I receive calls from therapists desperately seeking immediate consultation about a high conflict divorce or custody case. By the time they find their way to me for help, they are often already in the quicksand. I do my best to help them maneuver through those sticky situations ethically. A lot of times they come away from those situations learning how to restructure their policies and protocols moving forward by updating their informed consent document, setting and observing important boundaries and implementing protocols in the future so that they never find themselves in that desperate situation again. It is my hope this book will provide an opportunity for you to be proactive and prepared.

By the end of this book you will have specific protocols you might put into practice. By reading and referring to this book you will learn to do the following:

- Screen potential clients carefully and know when and who to refer out to other professionals.

- Have a comfortable understanding of the signs and signals of potentially problematic personality traits in parents of child clients.

- Learn how to spot *intractable dynamics* between parents and know how to navigate strategically.

- Obtain very thorough informed consent including a detailed signed policy on divorce and custody related cases.

- Know your role and inform parents initially and ongoing as to what your role is and what it is not.

- Create and observe a strict policy of no recording of your therapy sessions.

- Learn how to spot potential signs of *estrangement, alienation* and *loyalty conflict.* Learn how to address these situations therapeutically and strategically.

- Know what to do when you are served with subpoenas.

- Know how to properly respond to phone calls from attorneys and guardians ad litem.

- Develop a goal-directed treatment plan and document ethically and mindfully in the case you and your clinical record end up in court.

- Learn how to utilize your treatment plan to anchor the focus of treatment and redirect parents to focus on your role as therapist and the purpose of the therapy.

- Be prepared for testifying in court if required.

- Develop and practice a plan for your own self-care to mitigate the stress of these kinds of cases and avoid burnout and compassion fatigue.

It is my hope that this book will help you to help the children of parents embroiled in high conflict divorce and custody cases. It is also my hope that this book will help you feel well equipped and empowered so that you will not find yourself dragged into the middle of warring parents.

CHAPTER 1

The Nature of High Conflict
Divorce & Custody Cases

LET'S BE CLEAR. Not all divorce and custody disputes are high conflict. It is normal for parents divorcing or divorced to have a certain degree of conflict. After all, it's most likely they are divorced or divorcing due to conflicting views and preferences about the way they each want to live life and raise their children.

It would be in error to assume every parent going through divorce is high conflict. Not every divorce case is going to be a hazard for you and your practice. There are many families going through divorce or who have been previously divorced who are delightful clients whom you'll easily be able to help. I know of many therapists who have been so burned by one high conflict divorce case that they no longer accept any new clients who are divorced or divorcing out of fear they will experience again what they experienced before. It's understandable but that need not be the case.

Prepared with particular policies and protocols, you can develop greater confidence as a clinician, and you will be able to take on divorce related cases with forethought, proper mindset and preparedness. I want you to learn how to listen and look for the information you need in order to be wise and discerning and I want you to have an ability to take careful note as to where a family is on *the divorce conflict continuum* so that you can make adjustments as needed to the course of treatment.

Prior to the mid to late 1990's, the nature of conflict within a divorce was generally seen as part of the natural course of a couple going through the painful process of breaking up a marriage. In 1994 Janet Johnston, PhD. published a ground-breaking article called High Conflict Divorce published in *The Future of Children*, a biannual academic journal out of Princeton University and the Brookings Institution, that focuses on providing policy makers with the best available information regarding programs and policies for children. This particular article laid a foundation providing a lens through which professionals such as guardians ad litem, custody evaluators, family law attorneys and mental health professionals could see the nature of high conflict divorce and the potential effects on children. Johnston set forth some new perspectives on the varying dynamics between parents divorcing and the effects on children, while debunking some of the theories that were widely floating around in the mental health and legal arenas dealing with divorce and custody matters.

Psychologist and Family Coach, Kathy Marshack categorizes three kinds of divorce: 1) business-like divorce, 2) friendly divorce, and 3) high-conflict divorce. Borrowing from that short list and her own descriptions, I have added my own additional categories to create what I call *the divorce conflict continuum.*

I will include Marshack's categories below along with my own additions to represent some of the variety of scenarios I have observed in *the divorce conflict continuum*. These descriptive categories will help you to assess the level of conflict between parents in order for you to have a greater view of the family system's experience in context and how it may be affecting the child for whom you are providing therapy.

The Divorce Conflict Continuum

Business-like divorce: With this kind of divorce, both parties accept that the marriage needs to come to an end. Parties are amicable and the divorce process is handled respectfully. There is conflict, but the couple manages to negotiate, navigate, and work through any such conflicts with a focus on solution. After the divorce, the parties no longer communicate except brief, business-like exchanges only as needed. As a therapist you will find that the parents communicate with you separately, taking turns bringing the child to therapy, and typically are compliant, non-emotional and cooperative with the therapy process. This couple probably won't seek co-parenting counseling because they generally adopt a parallel, respectful parenting plan with very little contact after the divorce is finalized. They simply have gone separate ways and remain civil and polite.

Friendly divorce: This kind of divorce happens when a couple agrees that the relationship has changed form and they can no longer have a happy or healthy marital relationship, but they both wish to remain friends. In a friendly divorce, the terms are typically agreed to with relative ease and those agreements are made without much conflict. This couple likely comes to divorce and parenting agreement on their own without the need of attorneys. They continue having a friendly relationship

21

after the divorce is finalized. This is often a great benefit to the children as the children are more readily able to adjust to the change in the structure of the family and are more easily able to maintain healthy, positive relationships with both parents. This is the ideal kind of case for you as a therapist because you can work with the entire family system easily as needed and the child typically adjusts to the changes more easily than in other kinds of divorce. The parents are usually both supportive of the therapy process. This couple would be very willing to attend co-parenting counseling, but they probably won't need to as they get along on their own just fine.

Dedicated but irritated divorce: This divorce is when a couple has the best of intentions to put the children first. Both are committed to maintaining focus on what is in the best interest of children. They have different parenting styles, different opinions about what is best, they no longer like each other, and they both become easily irritated by the other. In these cases, the parents can be redirected and are willing to compromise for the best interest of the child. They are willing and able to hear from the therapist what they can and should be doing differently as parents. They want to improve. They have solid ego-strength, and they typically go to their own therapy and are each working on their own individual challenges and issues. This couple is willing to attend co-parenting counseling and can benefit.

Normal conflicted divorce: This couple's conflict is considered normal during a divorce, and they may experience normal levels of mild conflict after the divorce is finalized. These parents will have some moderate emotional flare-ups with one another from time to time and sometimes flare in front of the children. These parents are able to return to calm and rational minds and reach resolution through compromise and negotiation.

They are typically compliant with the protocols and boundaries you set forth in the process of providing therapy to the child. They usually respect the process of therapy for the child. This is a couple who will greatly benefit from co-parenting counseling services with another professional, and they are open and willing to go.

Habitual fight-mode divorce: With this family, the divorced or divorcing couple will always have conflict because their manner of communication and resolving conflict involves raised voices and emotional tension. They often come from family history where fighting and yelling was simply part of the reality. This couple has likely always argued and fought as a habitual part of their relationship dynamic and communication style. The child has grown up hearing the parents fighting since birth. In a way, fighting in this family feels normal for them. With this family you will be working a lot to help the child develop healthy assertiveness skills, non-violent communication, skills, and you'll be setting boundaries with the parents so they do not pull you into their fights. The level of conflict is differentiated from a high conflict divorce because through the fighting they often come to agreements and compromise even if they arrive at this through blustery and heated exchanges. The parents in this family don't hate each other and they usually care deeply for their children so they will be compliant with bringing the children to you for therapy. You can refer this couple to co-parenting counseling, but it may not be helpful to them as their behavior is so hard-wired.

High conflict divorce: In these cases, the couple is incapable of finding resolution to subjects of disagreement without high levels of hostility, anger and often full-blown hatred. This kind of divorce and the high level of negative emotional energy can consume one or both partners. It causes damage not only to the couple's ability to relate to one another, but it damages the children, other family members and sometimes spills over into the community as the warring parents drag friends, neighbors, other professionals and extended family into their battles. These are the cases that can deplete a therapist's energy-stores and drain a therapist's time if policies and protocols are not consistently observed. While normally involving the parents in consideration of family system dynamics is important, with the truly high conflict cases you may find it wise to observe limited communication with the parents beyond the requisite intake procedure, updates on progress and parenting recommendations made equally to both parents. If you allow for open and frequent interaction with these parents, the intractable dynamics and high levels of emotion these parents exhibit will likely interfere with your ability to provide effective therapy for the child. You will refer this couple out for co-parenting counseling, but they may never actually go. If they do go to co-parenting counseling, it's unlikely it will be helpful due to the intractable dynamics. With these parents it can feel impossible to provide any direct help for the parents, and it can feel at times hopeless in terms of assisting the child.

The research shows that when there is a high level of intense and hostile conflict between parents focused on the child and witnessed by the child, it is a reliable predictor that the child will suffer mental and emotional adjustment problems (Amato, Loomis, & Booth, 1995; Buchanan, Maccoby, & Dornbusch. 1991; Buehler et al., 1998; Cummings & Davies, 1994; Grych & Fincham, 1993; Kelly, 2000; Kline, Johnston, & Tschann, 1990; Vandewater & Lansford, 1998).

Children of parents with high levels of conflict benefit from their own therapy to work through the strain and stress of living with their parents' dynamics. Children can benefit tremendously from therapy in these kinds of cases as long as your boundaries and professional protocols are enforced consistently with the parents. If a child is fortunate enough to receive quality therapy support in a high conflict situation, it is essential for the therapist to preserve that therapeutic relationship. You have an opportunity to provide one place where the child is able to feel heard, seen and encouraged to safely explore, experience and express all and any emotions. The therapy helps the child to develop coping skills for living in the tough circumstances of having parents who are at war with one another.

According to Janet Johnston (1994) there are three *dimensions of conflict* with a divorce which I have paraphrased here to provide a clear guideline and to lend to my own concept of continuum of divorce conflict:

- THE SUBJECT of the conflict (i.e. where the child will spend holidays, where the child attends school, who will pay for child-care, who keeps the dog after divorce).

- THE WAY the couple expresses and demonstrates conflict (i.e. yelling, angry emails, polite disagreeing discussion, through attorneys).

- THE DEGREE of negativity and/or hostility (i.e. subtle such as body language or eye rolls, moderate such as bad-mouthing one another to others or extreme such as cursing at one another in front of the children, threats, stalking).

It is normal for a couple going through the process of divorce to have conflicts about finances, household items and decisions about the children up until the final divorce decree is signed. But when the conflict chronically persists at high levels after the divorce is finalized, causing problems for the family's healthy functioning, or when there is an extreme variance in the manner and the degree of hostility, it is quite possible that there are elements of pathology (Johnston, 1994).

When we see signs of possible pathology, we need to shift the way we go about conducting the process of therapy — adjusting our methods of communicating with the parents and ensuring implementation of protocols and boundaries. It is important for therapists to remember that we are not diagnosing parents. We are using our skills of clinical discernment to note when there are traits and behavioral elements that may inform how to go about doing our job as the child's therapist with the goal of maintaining our proper role and preserving the integrity of the therapeutic process. I caution therapists not to go down the diagnostic path when noting potential pathology in parents. It's important to only use these indicators to inform and assist in the process of shaping an effective treatment plan.

I want to share with you about a time in my own career where I erred and, as a result, I learned how to handle these kinds of cases differently and more effectively. When I reflect on that time in my career in which I had a cluster of high conflict divorce cases, I can see where I failed to identify the signs and signals of pathology in parents early enough. At that time in my professional development, I avoided using a pathological lens as a matter of principle. I wanted to believe that if I could help parents see how their behavior was causing emotional harm to their children, I would be able to appeal to a core of rational goodness that I believed was deep inside of every person. That optimistic perspective was misplaced and mistaken in these particular cases.

This way of thinking and believing as a clinician was in error because in reality these very high conflict situations, most often involve parents so consumed by rage, obsessive hatred and need for vengeance that they are incapable of seeing that their attitude, words and behavior are harmful to the children. Their pathological traits prevent them from taking any responsibility or ownership for the issues at hand. With 20/20 hindsight, I have been able to reflect and see clearly that those particular parents were not capable of being rational. My attempts to appeal to the core of goodness I believed to be within them only made it harder for me to observe boundaries that would have better preserved my ability to provide ongoing effective therapy for the children. Thankfully, I had excellent mentorship from seasoned supervisors and peers that helped me to swiftly shift gears and make clinical decisions best for the child clients by adjusting the treatment plans to include more formalized and carefully structured interactions with the parents. If I could turn back the hands of time with those cases, I would have identified the yellow and red flags early on, set my boundaries more firmly from the beginning and followed all of the protocols I will be sharing with you in this book.

Parents who are experiencing normal degrees of conflict within the divorce process, absent of pathology, are usually able to accept therapeutic redirection and demonstrate ownership of their behavior. When there are signs of potential pathology present, efforts to redirect a parent's behavior will likely not only be ineffective but may cause a parent to turn their rage toward you or worsen the situation for the child.

Parents who come charging out of the gate in the first phone call with you, or during the parent intake session, are presenting flags. You need to pay attention to those flags. When parents present with high levels of hostility toward and about the other parent, show inability to self-regulate, or disregard your efforts to redirect them, you are seeing clear signs that should not be ignored.

In the process of discerning whether a family is experiencing a high conflict divorce or another point on the conflict continuum, it's important to remember that sometimes parents will report to you on the front end that they are having an amicable divorce, but as the divorce progresses, conflict develops and sometimes everything goes sideways. Normal levels of conflict may suddenly spike far beyond normal. Under the stress of it all, sometimes parents' behavior and presentation may go from compliant and cooperative to defiant and consumed with anger or inability to self-regulate.

When people experience an extreme level of stress with the process of divorce, it is not uncommon for a person to have temporary mood swings and behavioral changes. When typical or normal, the parent will eventually be able to return to calm and will most often express regret and distress about having felt out of control or out of bounds. When there is a pathological component, there will likely be persistence of the hostile behavior over time without remorse or apology. This is something we will go over in greater depth in Chapter 4.

It's wise to consistently follow most of the policies and protocols you'll learn in this book with all clients who are divorced or divorcing. The exception is when a family is not experiencing high conflict you can successfully include the parents more in the therapy. Being clear, firm, and consistent with your policies and protocols is absolutely the key to being able to provide therapeutic support without being dragged into the parents' warring dynamics.

CHAPTER 2

Initial Screening

WHEN YOU ARE on the phone for the first time with a parent of a potential child client, this is your golden opportunity to:

1. Gain and gather valuable information to help you discern if this family is a good fit for you and your practice.

2. Screen for yellow and red flags.

3. Establish important boundaries around your protocols and policies.

4. Explain your role.

5. Begin establishing rapport to pave the way for a therapeutic relationship built upon understanding, cooperation and respect for the process of therapy.

Imagine that you have received a voicemail from a mother requesting therapy support for her daughter. You return the call after you are finished seeing your clients for the day. How will you structure this initial call in order to achieve the above objectives?

For the purpose of this example and for the sake of simplicity, we will pretend this is a female parent divorcing a male parent calling you. The protocol would be the same regardless of parental gender.

It's a good idea to always inform the parent at the beginning of the return call as to how much time you have for this initial conversation. Let her know that you may have to interrupt if it looks like the time is getting short. Tell her you want to be sure you get her all the information she needs before the end of the call. This in itself begins the process of setting clear boundaries and expectation for respecting your time.

Begin with a warm open-ended request for information. Here is an example:

"I understand you've called seeking support for your daughter. Can you tell me a little bit about what's going on for her and your family?"

Asking an open-ended question like this will often result in the parent launching into a long explanation which will provide you a lot of valuable information. Just be sure you are ready to interrupt to redirect, if needed. You might try something like this if the parent is long-winded:

"Excuse me, I'm sorry to jump in and interrupt you but it does sound like there is a great deal of really difficult and complicated things going on for your family. . . Since we only have about 8 more minutes, I do want to be sure we have time for me to talk with you about how I can best help you. So, I want to give you a bit of information here..."

From here, you can redirect the conversation to presenting information about your services and your policies and procedures, or you can provide referral information if deemed appropriate. If you feel the information presented indicates this case is outside of your scope of expertise and training, or if it is right out of the gate sounding like an extremely complex and potentially draining case for you and where you are in your professional work, it will be best to provide referral options. You can explain supportively, *"I want to be sure you and your family are getting the most optimal attention and care. While I am not going to be the right therapist for your family, I do have several colleagues who will likely be a good fit. Let me provide their names and contact information."*

When you are listening and still in information-gathering and screening mode, it's important that you listen very carefully for what the parent *is* saying and also for what she is *not* saying. Notice her demeanor, her manner of communication, and level of emotion. Look for signs of stress in the way she communicates and the words she chooses. Listen for how she explains the child's symptoms and anything she volunteers about the child's family situation. Notice if she goes straight to speaking negatively about the child's father. If she does not come right out and share about marital status or family issues, be sure to ask directly like this:

"Can you tell me please who else is living in the home?"

Or

"Tell me a bit about your daughter's relationship with her father and siblings."

If she volunteers that there is another parent in the home, ask directly how the parents are getting along. If she tells you the other parent doesn't live in the home, ask if there has been a divorce.

If you learn that there has been a divorce, this is your cue to prepare to present your protocols and policies with regard to working with families when there is a divorced or divorcing situation. Something like this:

"I have very specific policies when I work with a family where there is a divorce. I have a special section in my initial paperwork I will review with you when you come in for the parent intake session. One of the things I will need to see prior to meeting your child is the most current standing court order that explains the current custodial situation. I have a second document that explains what my role is and what my role is not as therapist for your child in the case of divorce, along with explanation of roles of other professionals that may be involved. In order for me to help you and your child's other parent have clarity as to how I can best help your child and family, I want to be sure you and your child's other parent understand that I am not a custody evaluator or a co-parenting counselor. My role would be solely to provide therapeutic support for your child and general parenting guidance to best support your child's progress."

This is an essential step in establishing your professional boundaries. After presenting this information, you will likely hear the parent respond with more information regarding the status of the divorce or any lingering custody conflict.

Yellow and Red Flags

Yellow flags are caution points signifying your need to watch and listen very carefully for more information. Red flags give you clear messages that you are most likely looking at a high conflict dispute between parents with probability there are pathological elements for one or both parents.

Let's look at some potential yellow and red flags:

Yellow Flags

- When the parent is vague about the child's family and living situation: Ask directly for more information.

- When the parent casually mentions the other parent is not part of the child's life: Don't allow the conversation to drift from here. Interrupt if needed to ask directly for more information about this.

- When the parent hints that the child isn't getting along with the other parent: Ask directly for more details about this.

- When the parent mentions casually that she is divorced from the child's father: This is a good time to introduce your policies and protocols.

- When the parent seems to want to rush to make the appointment and get the child in right away: Slow down the conversation. Ask as many questions as you need to and provide information on your policies and protocols.

- When the parent seems highly emotional on the phone: Compassionately provide reassurance, time and space to see if the parent is able to self-regulate so you can ask questions and gather information.

- When the parent is overly familiar and too friendly with you as if they've known you as a close friend for years in the first conversation: Proceed as the professional you are. Do not fall into that false familiarity trap. You will need to inquire and collect information about the situation to determine if this client is a fit for you and your practice.

Red Flags

- When the parent is overtly bitter and hostile.

- When the parent discloses they are in the midst of a custody battle.

- When a parent is blatantly rude and dismissive of your professional boundaries during the first call.

- When the parent is so highly emotional they seem unable to self-regulate.

- When a parent discloses they've been diagnosed with a particular personality disorder.

When you spot yellow flags, ask further questions. Dig a little deeper. If you do not have time to do so during that initial call, I recommend you schedule a second phone call before scheduling an intake. Be sure to screen very thoroughly, but do not jump to conclusions too quickly, remembering that sometimes parents are simply having the normal symptoms of stress that go along with a divorce situation, and given some time they may demonstrate ability to self-regulate and receive your boundaries and redirection. It is best to remain compassionate, while at the same time maintaining your role and boundaries therein. You are, in effect, beginning the process of training parents how to be with you in the therapeutic process from that very first call.

When you spot red flags, you need to consider whether you have the energetic and temporal band-width to take on the case. A high conflict divorce or custody case can be a very challenging, yet rewarding experience if you are well prepared, have the chops and have the time it will demand. If your caseload is already full of challenging cases or you are going through a stressful time in your own personal life, you may want to refer out this case to another professional.

Chapter 3

How to Conduct the Parent Intake

ONCE YOU HAVE conducted the initial call and decided to accept the case, you will need to set up your initial parent intake(s). I realize my recommendations herein may not fit with the limitations or parameters of some managed healthcare systems. These recommendations I am making will likely work for therapists who are not paneled with insurance companies or managed health care systems, but they also can be adapted for therapists who are working within the managed care systems.

Ideally, it is a good idea to have all parent intake sessions be longer than a typical therapy session, preferably 90 minutes if plausible. The longer session will allow you an opportunity to review the informed consent in detail, the protocols and policies, clarification of your role and the business aspects of the therapy process. This longer session will also allow time for the parents to openly and fully share all current information about family dynamics and symptoms as well as a full history for the child and the family.

In terms of policies and protocols with families who are divorced or divorcing, I have a long list of items I include in my own informed consent that I review aloud with parents in the intake session. I recommend you adopt policies and protocols similar to these I am sharing and be sure to review your policies verbally with parents in the intake session. As you do, you may want to have them physically initial and sign along the way including a clause at the end that confirms they have had these policies and information about treatment explained and have had opportunity to ask questions. I recommend you have an attorney review your policies and informed consent in full to receive guidance from a legal perspective.

Here are some of my own policies you may use as a guide for creating your own:

1. Explain your role as therapist. Establish a clear stand that you are not a custody evaluator and, therefore, cannot provide any recommendations or commentary on anything related to a child's physical or legal custodial situation.

2. If a legal separation or divorce has occurred, require a copy of the most current standing court order demonstrating custodial rights for each parent/guardian, including all parts of any legally binding parenting agreement PRIOR to seeing the child for therapy. Review this court order with the parent(s) present in the intake session and establish who has primary physical custody and who has legal custody specific to health-related final decision-making authority. Note if the parents share legal custody. Depending upon the laws in your state or province, you may have legal obligation to both parents equally. (*Seek legal advice from an attorney in the state or province in which you live*). The reason this policy is so important is that you do not want to see a child for

therapy services based only on the information presented to you by one parent in the case a second parent has differing information or if the respective rights of each parent are unclear to you. If there is a legal document signed by a judge providing an outline of parental rights, you want to be sure you are upholding whatever is necessary and legally appropriate in your state. Additionally, it is important for you to have a full understanding of what a child's familial situation is, and these legal documents are a piece and part of your clinical understanding of the family system. Retain a copy of the court order in your clinical record. If there is any question with interpreting the legal documents, it is best to pay for a legal consultation with an attorney and create a note in the record as to how you are advised by that attorney.

3. Explain that you will need to obtain written, signed consent to treat a child in therapy from both legal parents/ guardians before seeing the child. Explain that you find it best to make every effort to include both parents in the therapy process and will need to have contact information for both parents prior to seeing the child. If the parents are divorced and the parent contacting you seeking therapy for the child has final decision-making on health-related issues, but the other parent does not want the child to attend therapy, you should consult with a supervisor and/ or an attorney and then use your best judgment. It is my own policy that in these cases I will not see the child if both parents will not provide informed consent because I do not want the child's therapy to be a point of heightened conflict or to be used in any future custody battle. I prefer to attempt to build rapport with both parents and invite a dissenting parent to hear me explain more about what

therapy will be like and how he or she can be a part of the process as a positive experience.

4. Set forth a policy that you will be communicating with both parents who share legal custody equally, encouraging both parents to participate in parent updates and progress review sessions throughout the process. Go on to explain that you will provide the same updates through a HIPAA compliant, encrypted email addressed to both parents with updates as to the progress of therapy as needed, and you will offer parent progress review sessions regularly naming the rate of frequency you prefer. Make it clear that if they wish to share information with you or ask you questions between sessions they can schedule a brief phone consultation for a designated fee and that if you hear from one parent, you will reach out to the other and allow the other parent equal opportunity to schedule with you. Remind both parents that any communications they have with you will be noted as part of the child's clinical record. Discourage parents from emailing you or including you on their emails to one another.

5. Explain that sometimes parent-child dyadic session, joint sibling sessions or family sessions in varying configurations may be recommended and that both parents will be informed and updated if so.

6. You may choose to provide a clause that states your policy of not testifying in court in order to preserve the integrity of your therapeutic alliance with the child client, and you may go on to ask they sign and initial specific agreement that they or their representatives will not subpoena you to court. You can further stipulate that if this policy is disregarded and you are subpoenaed and required to go to court your fee will be $____ (*typically more than what*

your regular fee is, but certainly seek your own legal guidance on what you can charge) for any and all court-related professional time. Specify that court-related time billed and charged typically is not covered by in-network or out-of-network insurance benefits. You can explain that you will provide an interview with a court-appointed guardian ad litem at the court-related fee and can prepare a summary of treatment for court purposes per your court fee if requested.

7. Provide clear explanation as to how your fees will be collected. You may wish to maintain one credit card on file if you have a HIPAA and PCI compliant means of doing so, and explain they will have to work out the reimbursement to one another on their own. Alternatively, you can require that the person who brings the child to therapy will provide payment at time of services. If you have a way to store separate credit cards that is HIPAA and PCI compliant, that certainly is an option. If you are on insurance panels, you'll need to bill according to the guidelines in your respective contracts.

8. Indicate a clear policy that no clients or parents of child clients are permitted to record your sessions, phone conversations, or any other communications without express, advance, written permission from all parties (therapist, both parents and child). It is my recommendation that you further stipulate that if a recording is obtained in violation of this policy, therapy will be terminated and that you require 4 final weekly sessions with a child in order to have appropriate closure with the child. Additionally, if a session or communications are recorded without prior written agreement signed by all parties, client/parent agrees that such recording will not be used as evidence in *any current or future* legal action.

If the parents have high levels of conflict, you most likely will want to conduct separate parent intake sessions. This will offer you an opportunity to hear both perspectives as to the child's presenting issues, the family dynamics and any other concerns both parents may wish to share. It will also provide you a fair chance to assess the entirety of the situation for this family.

It is important for you to use the parent intake session as your opportunity to demonstrate that you are the professional who is guiding and directing the process of therapy. The structure in this first session helps to set that tone. Provide a firm handshake and a warm smile upon first meeting. Conduct yourself as the consummate professional that you are. Be warm and receptive. Be poised with upright posture. Explain to parents what to expect during this intake session by setting an agenda. Here is a sample of what you might say:

First, we are going to carefully review this informed consent document aloud and you will have opportunity to ask any questions you may have. We will take care of payment here at the beginning of session also so we can get the business of setting up our therapeutic framework before we dive into the details of why you are bringing your child for therapy. After that, you'll have an opportunity to talk with me about anything and everything related to your child's and family's situation. I will be asking some questions and in this first session, I will be taking some notes so I can be sure I remember all you are sharing with me in order to best help your family. Finally, I will explain to you how child therapy works and what you can expect from the therapy process, and I'll provide you a brief tour of the play room and the facilities.

By setting an agenda for the session, you have made it clear that you will take the reins if things get off track. You have also set the tone that says you are the professional and the authority over this therapy process.

Establish the structure of therapy. Explain there will be an initial phase of observational assessment and explain how that works in your practive. Set forth clear expectations for parental participation including clear policies with regard to communicating between sessions and meeting for parent consultations regularly and as needed. Speak to parents about the treatment planning process including how you will establish goals and objectives for therapy that will be a combination of your therapeutic judgment as well as parents' and child's input. Let parents know you will be reviewing progress according to the treatment plan with them ongoing and explain the manner in which this will take place.

With high conflict divorce cases, I recommend scheduling the child's sessions the same time and day on a weekly or bi-weekly basis to cut down on room for conflicts between the parents to flare. Come to an agreement as to when an ideal day and time will be, and stay true to that regular appointment time and date.

Finally, utilize this first parent session to establish the importance of focusing on the best interest of the child at all times, and encourage both parents to act as team players with you to support the child's progress in therapy.

CHAPTER 4

Parents: Behavioral Traits, Potential Pathology & Strategies

PARENTS PLAY A very important part in the process of therapy for children. Parents are most often the *legal* client to whom you have legal and ethical obligation. The parents of your child client are inevitably a major factor and influence with your child client's emotional and mental health. You are required to obtain informed consent from the legal guardians of your child clients. You have responsibility to provide updates on a child's progress in therapy to the parents. The legal guardians of your child clients have access to the clinical record. The parents usually are the ones bringing the child to therapy. In order to help parents remain invested in the process of therapy, you have to build and maintain rapport with the parents as well as the child.

Ideally, parents will participate in and support the process of therapy as team players in between sessions and in parent sessions. We always want to involve and help the entire family system for best therapeutic outcome whenever possible. But when parents who are engaged in high conflict divorce demonstrate particular behavioral traits that indicate possible pathology, it is important to implement strategies in order to preserve the therapeutic process.

In general, it's always important to stay clear of diagnosing or vilifying parents, even in your own mind. Remain aware of any tendency you may have to jump to conclusions, assign labels, or categorize a parent too hastily. Watch out for countertransference that can be problematic for the therapeutic process, and seek supervision or consultation if it seems to be a challenge for you. Do not diagnose parents; but do utilize your diagnostic knowledge to help you strategize how you might ensure rapport, trust, and appropriate boundaries are in place so the child and family can best be helped and supported.

Elements of Behavior that MIGHT Point to Pathology in Parents

- *Splitting behavior*

- *Poor boundaries*

- *Rigidity*

- *Mood swings*

- *Extreme swings in energy levels (manic – depressed)*

- *Exaggerating/Grandiosity*

- *Lying or deceptive behavior*

- *Explosive behavior*

- *High hostility and/or rage*

- *Extreme anxiety*

- *Depressed mood*

- *Inappropriate social behavior*

- *Obsessive/Compulsive*

- *Histrionic display*

In my experience there are generally seven common personality types that are particularly challenging. Here is a run-down of the seven I have nick-named for reference in consultations:

Helicopter Parent

- Overly protective/hovering

- Doesn't want child to go to play room without parent

- Enmeshment

- Frequently bringing child to therapy due to child anxiety which is due to their own anxiety

- Highly anxious

- Parent lacks awareness that his/her high anxiety is contributing to enmeshment and anxiety in child

Drama Mama/Papa

- Dramatic behavior and extreme emotional expressions

- Often looking for a diagnosis for the child

- Often assumes the worst case is true

- Poor ability to regulate emotions

- Often highly anxious, may even present as panicked

- Poor boundaries

- Sends you frequent, lengthy voice-mails and emails.

- Seems to thrive on chaos or drama

Drill Sergeant

- Overly controlling

- Operates from anger

- Yells often

- Quick to criticize, find fault

- Threatens and punishes regularly

- Resists therapy and resists "modern day parenting"

- Might say things to you such as, *"My parents hit me with a belt and I turned out just fine."*

Over-Sharer

- Wants to tell you every detail beyond what you need to know

- Sends long emails, leaves long voicemails, texts you with overly-detailed updates

- Poor boundaries

- Socially inappropriate, may be too personal in commentary

Lackadaisical Parent

- Drops child off at therapy

- Doesn't show up on time or no-shows frequently

- Won't schedule parent sessions

- Unmotivated

- Doesn't follow through

- Unresponsive to your direction

- Doesn't do any of the suggested homework activities between sessions

- Maybe seems depressed, anxious

Sneaky & Manipulative

- They have an agenda

- Pretending/False behavior/ Disingenuous

- Lying, deceptive

- Litigious, court-involved

- Have underlying motivation for bringing child to therapy to get help

Splitting Parent:

- Vacillates between telling you"You're the BEST.... You're the WORST"

- Overly charismatic

- Overly complimentary

- Overly critical

- May swing between euphoric about you and therapy to disdainful

- Talk to you about things that have nothing to do with the child and the therapy

- Easily "injured," feeling snubbed or rejected for no reason

- Often there is an agenda/underlying motivation for bringing child to therapy

As you encounter challenging personalities or behavioral traits that may point to pathology in parents of child clients, it's wise to have a set of strategies. Here are ten strategies I recommend:

Strategy #1: Screen for red flags and know when to refer out.

- Know yourself. Know your personal triggers and risks of unhealthy countertransference. Seek your own therapy and supervision.

- As discussed previously, use that first phone call to cast your net for information with open-ended questions and listen carefully for what is said and for what is not being said.

  1. Divorced?

  2. Tension between parents?

  3. Speaks negatively about the other parent?

  4. Hints about suspicions regarding sexual abuse?

  5. Is the parent's speech pressured?

  6. Does the parent act too familiar with you? Too friendly beyond polite?

Strategy #2: Seek to understand.

- Try to understand the history and context for what contributed to this parent's behavior.

- Spend time in the intake and parent sessions gathering family history.

- Create a genogram and look at the whole dynamic through a family systems perspective.

- Work to feel empathy and compassion for the parent while maintaining your boundaries.

- Ask open ended questions.

- Show genuine curiosity and reflect with empathy.

Strategy #3: Have very clear policies and protocols and stick to them.

- Require a copy of the standing court order demonstrating parental rights before seeing the child if there is a divorce.

- Be clear on your policy about going to court.

- Clarify your policy on scheduling & cancellation.

- Be clear on your fees, including time spent reading emails beyond a line or two and on time spent on the phone.

- Explain policy around parents remaining in the waiting room during session and no cell phone conversations while waiting.

- Do not allow recording of sessions.

- Requirements around parenting sessions and updates on child's progress.

Strategy #4: Establish your role and repeat as needed.

- "My role is therapist for your child and I am here to assist your child through his process of healing and growth."

- "My role is to provide parenting guidance and recommendations as it relates to your child's healing and growth during the play therapy process."

- "My role is to be unbiased and fair with both parents of your child."

- "My role is not to make custody recommendations in any way."

- "My role is not to be your child's advocate in your battle with the school."

- "My role is mandated reporter in the case I have reason to believe any child has been harmed or is in danger."

- "My role is not to investigate or determine whether a child has been harmed by someone."

Strategy #5: Build trust and rapport from the beginning and don't go head to head.

- In line with the second strategy of seek to understand and have empathy, it's important – *especially when a parent's behavior is irritating* – to remember your goal is to maintain trust and rapport with the parent as much as possible.

- Find ways to express observations, questions and recommendations in a way that doesn't cause the parent to get defensive.

- Reassure parents you don't ever want to make them feel "wrong."

- Express curiosity inviting parents to help you figure out what may be going on even if you very well know what is really going on.

- Don't confront head on. If they confront you in a harsh manner, maintain your boundaries firmly but softly.

Strategy #6: Keep your focus and the focus of the therapy on the child's needs and progress.

- When parents try to derail the focus of the therapy, get off topic, make it about something else, manipulate or try to dominate your time, REDIRECT parents to why we are here and what the focus is.

- From the beginning, establish the flow of how sessions will be conducted, and don't allow the child's play therapy session time to be interrupted or overridden by an over-bearing parent demanding to speak with you privately.

- Set up separate parenting consultation for a fee. Don't let them get into a trend of calling you or emailing you without paying for your time.

Strategy #7: Find neutral gear and practice shifting into neutral when needed.

- Practice neutral facial expression, body language and tone in the mirror at home.

- Train yourself to shift into neutral when others escalate.

- Feel your feet firmly on the ground and hold your head high.

- Remember this parent's high emotion is about them and not about you.

- If a parent comes across aggressively toward you, don't defend or react. Calmly refer to your policies as needed.

Strategy #8: Stick to the treatment plan. Refer to the treatment plan. Review the treatment plan regularly.

- With difficult parents your treatment plan is your anchor.

- Include them in the plan for treatment from the beginning and ongoing.

- Refer to it when you need to remind them why we are here.

- Review the plan and the progress or lack of progress frequently to frame the recommendations you are making.

Strategy #9: Document everything and seek supervision.

- In the case of the occasional malignant or threatening personality, it's best to have a very careful record of all communications, correspondence and concerns.

- In the clinical record, be cautious about the words you choose. Keep it very clinical in the record using clinical descriptions documenting the parent's behavior. (*i.e. Mother brought client to session. Mother appeared highly agitated and preoccupied. OR i.e. Father appeared angry per facial expression and volume of voice when I declined his demand to sit in on child's therapy session per policy. Father's anger escalated and he slammed a door when leaving the office*).

- Schedule supervision sessions with a seasoned therapist who can serve as a support and witness to your treatment of the client in case the difficult parent later makes accusations that have to be defended.

- Seek further case consultation with seasoned peers, and request they document the consultation in case needed.

Strategy #10: Talk about termination from the very beginning with parent and client.

- Be sure to have a clause in your informed consent about requirement of 4 closure sessions with child in the case the parent should decide to end therapy abruptly prior to or against therapist's recommendation.

- Cover the importance of appropriate closure of the therapy process and relationship being a *process* and that it can cause harm to a child to abruptly pull the child out of a relationship they've established with the therapist.

- Be prepared for abrupt termination due to parents pulling child from therapy to happen by finding way to let the child know that one day they won't be coming here to play. Create a ritual where at the end of each session the child and you name something that was pleasant or helpful from the session that day and write it on a clothes pin or a rock to add to a collection at home to help the child remember when needed and so she can always remember the pleasant and helpful times she had in therapy with you.

Bonus strategy/tips:

- Look for the child's strengths and emphasize these strengths to the parents in order to overcome parents' tendency to blame the child or focus on the child's deficits.

- Avoid clinical jargon (i.e. instead of using the word "*dysregulated*" you might say "*Your child seems to have a hard time managing intense emotions.*"

When you have a high conflict divorce case, whether or not there is actually pathology, you will most likely encounter personality and behavioral traits in one or both parents that will present a

challenge for you. It is very important to be prepared with prac-
ticed strategies. It is essential to maintain your ground as the
professional. Remind parents you are there to provide therapy
and support for the child and, in extension, for the family as a
whole. When a parent's behavior makes it difficult for you to
support the family system directly, you will want to zoom in
on your work with the child and help the parents' behavior not
to interfere with your therapeutic process by employing the
strategies provided in this chapter.

Chapter 5

Identifying Intractable Dynamics & Adjusting the Treatment Plan

Intractable dynamics can spur from the emotions and behavior of one or both parents, with the child or with the parents and child in concert due to some level of mental health challenge and vulnerability due to the high stress of the division of the family (Friedlander & Walters, 2016). When the intractability is identified solely within the relationship between the parents, Friedlander & Walters (2016) determined that mental health challenges are frequently at the root of these dynamics, as the parent with pathology projects the entirety of the conflict onto the other parent, incapable of owning any part of the problem. Often these cases are a result of something Friedlander & Walter identify as *encapsulated delusion,* during which one parent is fixated on an irrational and unsubstantiated belief that the other parent has somehow harmed or abused the child (2016).

When you are able to observe that one or both parents seem stuck in a rigid and accusatory view of the other parent, you can be assured you are likely observing intractable dynamics. And when there are intractable dynamics, there is often interference with the healthy therapeutic process by one or both parents, as there is most often some underlying pathological motivation and agenda. Often, in these cases, you will note the child is rejecting and refusing contact or connection one parent.

These dynamics are extremely complex and it is wise for you to practice the strategy of anchoring into your role as the child's therapist and honing in on the treatment plan, making adjustments as needed. When one parent is rigid in their belief that the other parent is all bad and all wrong, it can be very difficult if not impossible to gain cooperation with your goal of helping the child to have positive and healthy relationships with both parents.

In these cases, it is often best to at least temporarily protect and preserve your therapeutic relationship with the child while creating some distance between that process and the parental involvement in therapy. This will allow you to provide the child an emotionally safe and secure space and relationship to explore and express all emotions without the watchful eye of the intractable parent.

At the same time, it is important to know that if one parent is being rejected by the child and time is going by without that parent and child talking or seeing one another, this can damage to the parent-child relationship in ways that may be irreparable. In these severely intractable dynamics, your treatment plan may need to be adjusted to include other professionals added to create a team to support this family.

These cases almost always involve attorneys, and a guardian ad litem or perhaps a custody evaluator. It is often advisable to add to your team other mental health professionals. You might recommend individual therapists for each parent and a very strong co-parenting therapist. Ideally, all professionals can then work together to ensure the best interest of the child and that those parent-child relationships are supported (Friedlander & Walters, 2016).

The treatment plan should be thoughtfully developed and reevaluated on a regular basis to ensure you are very clear as to the goals of the therapy you are providing, the measurable objectives you are working to achieve and the specific interventions you are utilizing to work toward those goals and objectives. The treatment plan is your cornerstone and anchor to which you will return and reference whenever the levels of high conflict between parents throws the course of therapy off-track. It is vital that a therapist knows at all times what the goals and objectives for treatment are. It can be very easy to be pulled in multiple directions with the commonplace crisis du jour that will undoubtedly arise as par for the course in these high conflict divorce cases where there are intractable dynamics.

When parents are so rigid in their irrational and unsubstantiated position that the other parent is all bad and all wrong, it is highly unlikely they are able to hear any rational direction, guidance, or recommendations you have to provide. You will have to find a work-around. You can remind the parent of the goals and objectives of the therapy, but this is more for the sake of your ability to stay anchored. Staying anchored in remembering your role, what you are here to do to support the child's best interest in therapy, is crucial to maintaining the integrity of the therapeutic process and for maintaining your own mental well-being. These intractable dynamics and, specifically, the behavior of rigid parents who may be experiencing *encapsulated delusion,* can produce a great deal of stress for a therapist. Leaning into your treatment plan and making adjustments to the interventions to serve the objectives and goals will help you mitigate the stress these cases can cause.

Again, one of the most helpful adjustments you may make to the treatment plan when there are these intractable dynamics is to implement a team of mental health professionals. I recommend that you encourage each parent to attend their own therapy, providing referral options. Obtain release and waiver allowing for each team member to confer in order to support mutual goals for best interest of the family as a whole. Co-parenting counseling may not work on its own, but if a solid co-parenting therapist can join the team of professionals, this can be a helpful piece to the treatment plan. It can be very difficult if not impossible for one therapist to provide everything the family needs when there are high levels of conflict and intractable dynamics. When you are able to bring together a team of professionals to support the family, this frees you to focus on your therapeutic relationship with your child client rather than having to manage the parent conflict on your own.

Chapter 6

Alienation, Rejection of a Parent & Loyalty Conflict

THE ORIGINAL CONCEPT of *parental alienation syndrome* proposed by Richard Gardner in 1984 was singularly focused on the efforts of one parent to program or brainwash a child against the other parent to the point the child would experience a pathological rejection of the alienated parent. Further studies that came out in the early 1990's showed that there can actually be many reasons a child will exhibit alienating behavior.

The idea of parental alienation as a syndrome or diagnosis has been extensively debated and dismissed in the literature due to the lack of empirical efficacy and the strategic use of the concept within custody disputes (Kelly & Johnston, 2001). What the research does support is that there can indeed be an *alienated child* defined by Kelly & Johnston (2001) as a child who openly and persistently expresses extreme negative emotions toward a parent that are clearly disproportionate to the experiences the child has had with that parent. An *alienated child* shows ongoing signs of unwavering rejection of a parent without any guilt or hesitation. Johnston carefully distinguishes the alienated child from a child who has been neglected or abused by a rejected parent (1994).

There are numerous normal developmental reasons a child might show preference for one parent over the other, and there is a continuum to be considered. That continuum ranges from a child having a positive relationship with both parents to the other extreme of being alienated from one parent. In between those two extremes, a child may simply have affinity for one parent over the other or may be allied with one parent while still loving the other parent (Kelly & Johnston, 2001).

Children who are estranged from one parent are differentiated from alienated children in that estranged children have witnessed or experienced abuse or neglect from the rejected parent. In these cases it is considered an expected and self-preserving response for a child to refuse contact with the parent.

When a child's parents are going through a divorce process, there is a lot of change happening for the child and it is normal for the child to demonstrate resistance to those changes. It's important for therapists not to jump to conclusions or automatically buy into one parent's accusations that the other parent is intentionally attempting to influence or brainwash a child.

Listen with caution and pause on judgments until you have had time to meet with both parents ongoing and work with the child directly. Remain as neutral as you can and remember your role as the child's therapist. Your job as a therapist for a child is to help and support that child through the challenges of a changing family and to be able to learn skills for respectful assertion, coping and self-regulation in the face of witnessing the parents' conflict.

As part of the process of case conceptualization and treatment planning, therapists need to have an understanding as to what the child's experience, emotions, beliefs and perceptions are from the child's perspective. If a child presents with persistent hostility and hatred toward one parent without reason and without regret, rejecting and refusing contact, this meets the criteria for an alienated child. Sometimes this results from a favored parent's campaign of degradation against the other parent and sometimes the favored parent has intentionally indoctrinated a child into believing the rejected parent deserves to be hated and rejected. It is important, however, to remember that it is not necessarily because the favored parent has been the direct cause of the alienation.

Loyalty conflict occurs internally for a child when the parents are experiencing ongoing high levels of conflict externally and the child is working to feel assured of love and acceptance from both parents (Lorandos et al., 2013). Often this *loyalty conflict* creates so much internal pressure that the child experiences cognitive dissonance, resulting in anxiety. Sometimes the child will align with one parent and reject the other in order to find relief. Think of it like the beach ball you try to push down and hold under water. Eventually, that ball will pop out one side or the other. Parents may unwittingly be pressing their child to choose sides. And in some cases, one parent very well may be intentionally pressuring a child to electively align with them.

It is my view that children are more vulnerable to alienation when they are lacking adult support outside of their warring parents. The therapy space with a qualified children's therapist can be an invaluable source of support to that child who otherwise cannot find relief from the unwitting or intentional pressurized home environment when the parents are going through divorce. Once children are alienated, engaged in that refusing and resisting behavior toward one parent, the child may be resistant to receiving therapeutic intervention because the process of therapy can trigger the underlying loyalty anxiety and can threaten the equilibrium they have managed to create through the rejecting and refusing behavior (Friedlander & Walters, 2016). It's important that the therapist develop authentic rapport with the child and allow for time to develop trust and comfort in the relationship before introducing directive therapy techniques.

Often, what will be required to implement a multi-professional team to treat these complex dynamics is a court order that carefully outlines the expectations of the whole family's treatment with collaboration among the mental health professionals that includes reporting to the guardian ad litem or the custody evaluator as to progress and prognosis along the way. It is common for families with high levels of conflict and intractability to be forced by a court order to participate in the complex level of treatment in order to see improvement and resolution (Friedlander & Walters, 2016).

There are more extreme interventions that may be implemented when a child is so severely alienated that the child fails to respond to the therapy process, or when the therapist notes progress in the therapy room only to see the child severely regress after returning to the preferred parent's home environment. Reunification therapy is another level of therapeutic intervention, and this requires special training. For the purpose of this book, I will not go into the details as I believe it is important for therapists to receive specialized training, supervision, and consultation in order to learn the complexities of options and methods of reunification therapy.

It is important to note that I normally advise therapists in supervision, training and consultation to work with the whole family system when helping a child in therapy. I normally do not advise children be treated without directly involving parents and siblings in sessions in order to promote systemic growth and healing. On the face of a case where a child is in a family that has such conflict it would seem to make sense to work with the entire family system. Given the consequences and context of severely intractable dynamics in high conflict cases, however, it is essential to preserve the therapy process for the child and refer the parents to other professionals for individual therapy and co-parenting counseling. It bears repeating for me to say again that these extremely complex cases are simply too much for one therapist to handle alone. It is wise to build a therapeutic team whenever possible. The child in these cases needs a therapist who is there to provide an emotionally safe distance from the war zone experienced at home and the child's therapist needs to be able to focus on maintaining that therapeutic experience without distraction and interference

It's important for a therapist who is working with a child in a high conflict divorce and custody dispute to know that when the dynamics are so intractable and the child is alienated and unresponsive to your therapeutic interventions, it is best to seek further in-depth supervision and consultation regarding the potential for reunification therapy, which will require a different compass, map and route.

CHAPTER 7

Attorneys, Guardians ad Litem & Subpoenas

IT IS ALWAYS helpful for me to remember that the family court arena and the mental health arena are two very different cultures. The norms and typical behaviors and tendencies of each arena can seem disparate, and in order to work together in a way that best serves the needs of children and families, we need to have a clear understanding of how to have effective and appropriate communication with attorneys and guardians ad litem.

Keep in mind that family law attorneys are hired by their clients to get the best outcome for those clients. While we are hired to help our clients heal, grow, and develop skills for healthier coping, communication and relationships, divorce attorneys are typically hired to go to battle for what their client feels they deserve and want from the divorce and custody dispute. While often attorneys from each side are able to help clients reach a settlement, most family lawyers are prepared to fight as needed in order to win the case.

It is my observation that the lawyer's brain is simply wired differently than the way a therapist's brain is wired. Attorneys often seem to process information in a linear, convergent way whereas therapist typically have a more multi-faceted, divergent process of obtaining and examining information as it is presented. Attorneys sometimes seem to speak a different language than we do as therapists. A lawyer's orientation is very different than the perspective you have as therapist. You, as a therapist, are most likely considering the best interest of a child's mental, physical and emotional well-being in the context of a family system. The attorney is hired to represent one of the parents in a divorce and custody case and is, therefore, focused on winning that case for his client. In order to win the case, the attorney will sometimes work to make the other parent look as bad as possible in the eyes of the court. While our aim as therapists is to help a family see each other with understanding and ideally work together positively and harmoniously, the aim of the lawyer is to win the case or to get their client's best outcome.

In my career I've encountered many very fair-minded attorneys who certainly are capable of focusing on the best interest of the children. The conflictual nature of divorce and custody litigation, however, doesn't leave a lot of room for attorneys to join us in our therapeutic orientation and mindset. When a therapist is able to understand the nature of the family lawyer's thought process and the expectations of the attorney's job, it can make it easier to understand why we as therapists need to have particular strategies in place for communicating with attorneys when necessary.

Ordinarily, guardians ad litem are also trained and practicing as family attorneys because attorneys are most familiar with the legal proceedings and the law. In some states, a guardian ad litem may be a trained volunteer or a psychologist though typically psychologists serve in a role of custody evaluator, which potentially involves formal psychological assessments and consideration to the psychological fitness of parents, as well as the psychological status and wellbeing of the children involved. Guardians ad litem who are attorneys most often do not have that psychological background or frame-work, and as a result, they often look to the therapist who is working with the family for guidance and direction as they conduct their investigation and prepare a recommendation for the court. This can create sticky territory for you.

The rules and regulations for guardians ad litem may differ from state to state, but by general definition a guardian ad litem is someone who is appointed by a court to represent the best interest of a minor child in a single court matter (Cornell, 2018). The role of guardian ad litem is one that can be somewhat vague in terms of what is required, depending on the state's statutes (Halikias, 2005). Sometimes there can be risk of gaps in communication between a therapist and guardian ad litem, as the guardian conducts his/her appointed duty of assessing and making recommendations to the court with regard to custody and related matters as to a child's best interest. It's important to have protocols for how you communicate with the guardian ad litem.

Ideally, a guardian ad litem will be unbiased, neutral and fully focused on what is actually in the best interest of a child. Unfortunately, sometimes guardians ad litem have some degree of bias toward one side's legal representation, or occasionally a guardian ad litem is unable to really hear and honor the professional perspective of the therapist working with the child and the family due to preconceived beliefs or ideas about the situation. In my own opinion, it has been better for the child and family when there is a psychologist appointed as custody evaluator on high conflict cases in addition to a guardian ad litem so that thorough understanding of the often complex psychological aspects of the dynamics, personalities and behavioral tendencies can thoroughly be folded into formal recommendations for the court.

That said, we must be prepared to do the best we can within the system in which we find ourselves working to support the best for our child clients and their families. Knowing how to be strategic in communicating with guardians ad litem and family attorneys can go a long way.

Know your state laws regarding privilege and confidentiality.

Be sure you are well-informed and able to recite the statute in your state law that requires you protect the privacy of your clients. The Health Insurance Portability and Accountability Act (HIPAA) is the United States' federal law protecting the privacy of healthcare information and is only superseded by more stringent state laws (HIPAA, 2016). If you are contacted by an attorney or a guardian ad litem, it is a good idea to have a standard statement with which you can reply that states, *"In accordance with my obligation per [your state's statute] and HIPAA, I am unable to confirm or deny the identity of any of my clients without written release and waiver or court order."* Your next step will be to contact the legal clients (parents of your child client) and inform them that you have received a call or letter from an attorney or guardian ad litem requesting information and that you have responded with the above. Remind your clients of their privacy rights, your obligations therein and your policies outlined in the informed consent document they signed and agreed to follow. Inform them if they would like you to respond to the attorney or guardian ad litem you will need them to sign your release and waiver form. Remind them that if you are subpoenaed to court, you may be required by a judge to breach their privacy, so it may be best for them to ask their attorney to allow you to be left out of the legal proceedings in order to preserve the integrity of the therapeutic relationship.

If it is a guardian ad litem contacting you, you can reply with the above but you might add, *"... If there is a court order extending you right to access me and my record with regard to a one of my clients, please forward a copy of that court order for my review and I will be happy to comply."*

It's advisable to always be very polite with attorneys and guardians ad litem while observing your professional boundaries at the same time. It's not a good idea to come across as terse, defiant, or stiff-arming with an attorney or guardian ad litem because if and when your client does release you to communicate, it's best to have good rapport with all other professionals involved with the family you are supporting in therapy.

If you obtain release and waiver from both legal parents to communicate with an attorney, be prepared to walk a careful line of willingness to be helpful, while protecting your therapeutic relationship with the child client and your clinical record. Ask the attorney a general open-ended question such as how you might be of assistance. Hear what the attorney has to say. If you are asked direct or even indirect questions regarding your opinion on anything related to custody, be prepared to assert clearly that your role is as therapist to the child, not as custody evaluator and that your ethics prohibits you from providing any opinion on custody matters. It's likely best to contain any information you share with an attorney to the goals of therapy and the general overview of your therapeutic interventions. Refrain from going into any details about the client, the family, or your experience in the therapy room. You might offer a general statement regarding the status and progress of therapy, staying away from specifics. It's best to steer clear of any details about the parents' behavior or presentation, keeping in mind you want to appear as neutral and unbiased as possible with focus on the child's therapy. Generally, this call with an attorney is likely a fishing expedition for the attorney to find out any information that will be helpful to his client's case and to learn how helpful you may be as a potential witness. Remember, the attorney is only doing his/her job. You can let attorneys know that you have all parents of all child clients sign an agreement that they will not subpoena you to court and that it is your intention to preserve the therapeutic relationship with your child client and that being involved in court has a tendency to disrupt and harm the integrity of the therapeutic relationship and process.

When a guardian ad litem has provided you a court order that shows the judge has made this appointment and specifically extended rights for access to a child's healthcare providers and any related healthcare records, you can provide the guardian ad litem with a formal meeting by phone or in person. In my own practice, I have always notified the parents of my child clients first and asked they provide signed release and waiver in addition, although it usually isnot be necessary.

You might provide the guardian ad litem a written summary of treatment that outlines the dates of treatment, presenting issues, treatment goals, plan for treatment and progress of treatment. This is typically greatly appreciated by guardians ad litem and can often preclude requests for the actual clinical record which you most often want to protect from being released. While you want to remain in a willing and helpful posture with the guardian ad litem, be cautious about getting too comfortable or casual in your discussion. Be prepared for guardians to ask you questions about your opinion to help in their investigating process and use the same explanation as above that you are not a custody evaluator and cannot provide recommendations on custody. Speak from your role and perspective of the therapeutic needs of your child client. You might choose to be more open with the guardian ad litem about the parents' participation and demeanor during the process of therapy but be cautious to not sound as if you are biased.

In the case you are subpoenaed to testify in court (more in Chapter 10 about this), you will likely want to speak with the attorney who is subpoenaing you about what information they are looking for you to provide on the stand, so that you can be prepared. Occasionally you will be subpoenaed by the guardian ad litem, and in this case it is also a good idea to find out in advance what questions will be asked of you.

CHAPTER 8

Parenting Guidance and Co-parenting vs. Parallel Parenting

Part of the job we have when working with a child in therapy whose parents are divorced or divorcing is to guide the parents in terms of their parenting of the child to support growth and healing for the child. There is a fine line here, and it is important not to allow a cross into the custody evaluation and recommendation realm. It is best to refer the parents out for co-parenting counseling with another professional and document that you've made that recommendation and whether they have followed that recommendation or not. It is best to provide identical parenting guidance to both parents and include the *Child's Bill of Rights When Parents are Divorced or Divorcing* (Guillen, 2013). There are many forms of this available. You can adapt this to what fits best for your own practice. Here is a very thorough version I have adapted from the one published by Lina Guillen, Esq.:

1. A child has a right to love and be loved by both parents and all members of the child's family.

2. Parents will not deny the child reasonable access to communicate with the other parent and relatives.

3. Neither parent shall speak or write derogatory remarks about the other parent to the child, or engage in abusive, coarse or foul language that might be overheard by the child.

4. Parents should not argue, negotiate or discuss adult legal or business matters in the presence or ear-shot of the child.

5. Neither parent will pressure, solicit or influence the child's view, opinion or position concerning legal proceedings between the parents.

6. Parents will allow the child to have and display photographs of the other parent (or both parents) if the child wishes.

7. Parents will refrain from expressing moral judgments to the child about the other parent's choice of values, lifestyle, social relationships, financial decisions or career status.

8. Parents will acknowledge positively to the child that the child has two homes, regardless of which home the child spends more time.

9. The parents shall both work to cooperate in sharing and supporting time and experiences with the child.

10. Neither parent will trivialize or discourage in anyway the relationship a child has with the other parent.

11. Neither parent will interrogate the child about the other parent nor will either parent discourage the child from speaking openly about the other parent.

12. Parents will not use the child as a messenger to communicate with the other parent.

13. Neither parent will say and do things to try to gain the child as an "ally" against the other parent.

14. Neither parent will encourage or instruct the child to be disobedient to the other parent, stepparents or relatives.

15. Neither parent will discuss child support or other financial issues with the child.

16. Neither parent will permit the child to be transported by a person who is intoxicated due to consumption of alcohol or illegal drugs.

17. Neither parent will smoke inside structures or vehicles occupied at the time by the child.

The idea of using a standard "bill of rights" for all divorced and divorcing parents whose child is in therapy with you is to provide a clear delivery of baseline rules of engagement to keep parents on track and help empower children to know what their rights are as well. The above bill of rights is good to review with parents. Below is an adaptation to the bill of rights I have used which is geared toward the child. I recommend using the one below with children and parents so that everyone is on the same page. You may want to give copies to the parents and child to be affixed to the refrigerator at each home. I utilize this in order to empower children to use the respectful assertiveness skills they learn with me in therapy when their parents exhibit behavior that violates the bill of rights. I ensure the parents are very familiar with the bill of rights from the beginning and use it as a reminder throughout the therapy process.

Here is my simplified, child-oriented version adapted from one version developed by Kathleen O'Connell Corcoran, MS, NCC, and the Family Center of the Conciliation Court of Pima County, Arizona (1991) and another version developed by Robert Emery,

Ph.D., professor at University of Virginia and author of several books for children and parents about divorce:

As a Child of Divorced or Divorcing Parents, You Have a Right To. . .

1. Love both of your parents and be loved by both of your parents without feeling guilty. Your parents should both encourage you to love the other parent.

2. Be protected from your parents' anger with each other. Your parents may have a hard time getting along with each other, but that is not your problem to fix. You should not have to hear your parents fighting.

3. Be kept out of the middle of your parents' conflict. You should not be made to feel you need to pick sides, be a messenger for either of your parents or hear your parents complain about the other parent.

4. Never be asked to keep secrets from either of your parents. It's not right for a kid to be asked by a parent to keep a secret from the other parent.

5. Never to feel you have to choose one of your parents over the other. There is plenty of love to go all the way around!

6. Not feel responsible for either of your parents' feelings. They are grown-ups and you're a kid! They need to get help and support from other grown-ups, not from you. It is not your job to take care of either of your parents.

7. Know well in advance about important changes that will affect your life; for example, when one of your parents is going to move or get remarried. These big changes should never be a sudden surprise to you.

8. Reasonable financial support during your childhood and through your college years.

9. Feel your feelings, to express your feelings, and to have both parents listen to how you feel with respect for your feelings.

10. Be a kid. You are not an adult and should not be involved in adult issues.

Co-parenting

Ideally, a child will benefit when two divorced parents are able to parent cooperatively and collaboratively. Co-parenting requires respectful and healthy ongoing communication between parents in order to discuss decisions about a child's education, health and activities as well as work together on parenting time, child-care and attending a child's special events. Often even those parents who have the best of intentions need help learning how to effectively co-parent. Co-parenting therapy with a skilled therapist can be a very positive adjunct to the therapy you are providing for the child. I almost always provide formal recommendation and referral for parents to enroll in co-parenting counseling. It is advisable to obtain a release and waiver from both parents in order to confer with the co-parenting therapist in order to share observations you have that may help the co-parenting counselor with that particular treatment plan.

Parallel Parenting

When there is a pervasive level of high conflict between parents that persists beyond the finalization of the divorce with intractable dynamics, it is usually best to observe a parallel parenting plan to help mitigate conflict for parents. With parallel parenting, the parents do not engage except through brief, business-like messaging using a system such as an online calendar and messaging system. With parallel parenting, parents do not interfere or intervene in the way the other parent chooses to parent the child at the other home (barring serious safety concerns). Typically, with parallel parenting, parents have an air-tight parenting agreement that clearly defines the parenting time schedule, as well as procedures for making major decisions regarding the child's health, activities, education and religion. There is normally language in the court order that says parents will confer on major decisions, and if they cannot come to an agreement, a designated final decision-maker will determine what will occur. All communications are established in writing, and any changes to the schedule have to be agreed upon in writing with a designated amount of advanced notice.

It is usually the guardian ad litem who makes a recommendation to the judge as to whether parents should be ordered to work toward co-parenting or observe parallel parenting. If you are asked by the guardian ad litem for your opinion, it is best to only report the dynamics you have observed based in factual events and patterns of behavior without any subjective opinion or judgment.

The parents and the guardian ad litem may benefit from hearing your clinical perspective on parenting recommendations that relate directly to the optimal mental and emotional wellbeing of the child you are treating in therapy. It's important to carefully walk the line, and don't step over into making any comments that relate to where the child lives, the child's schedule with parents, or any topics that relate to the custodial situation.

CHAPTER 9

Treatment Planning & Record Keeping

I$_\text{T'S}$ ETHICALLY ESSENTIAL to maintain *all* clinical records with great attention and timeliness. When it comes to high conflict divorce and custody cases, it is wise to maintain your clinical record, keeping in mind your clinical record very well may be subpoenaed and submitted into evidence in court. Clean, clear, mindful treatment planning and record keeping with high conflict cases is very important.

Treatment Planning

Your treatment plan is your anchor and your map that will keep you and the families with whom you work on track. I am a strong proponent of goal-directed treatment planning with measurable objectives and specific interventions in alignment with the objectives and goals based upon the most current research and peer-reviewed literature to support your plan rather than drifting through the therapeutic process, putting out fires as they pop up. High conflict divorce and custody cases carry a combustibility risk. Orienting your focus on clean, clear and mindful treatment planning is the way to mitigate those risks and protect the best interest of your child client and your own liability.

The word *diagnosis* comes from a Greek word meaning *to distinguish* or *to discern* (Dictionary, 2018). A diagnosis when working with child clients whose parents are experiencing high conflict divorce and custody disputes should be utilized as a pointer and a basis for how to develop the treatment plan but never a close-ended label. It is best when developing the diagnosis to consider three overarching elements of consideration, revisiting throughout the course of therapy. Those three areas to consider carefully are: 1) Biopsychosocial, 2) Developmental, and 3) Temporal. In consideration of the biopsychosocial factors, you are looking at the child and family's physical, social and psychological health/wellness, along with family history. When giving consideration to the developmental factors, you are examining where the child is in terms of social, mental and physical development relative to what is considered normal or abnormal for the child's age. In looking at temporal factors, you are considering the timing and context of presenting problematic emotions and behaviors.

Documenting your intake of information from parents and your child client, along with all of your observations that go into your assessment process helping you arrive at a working diagnosis, you can then begin to develop your treatment plan. Overall, you want to be prepared to easily and clearly explain to parents, to the guardian ad litem and to the court exactly what you are doing and why you are doing it. It is simply unwise – and many would argue also unethical – to fly by the seat of your pants, estimating and using trial-by-error methods session to session when you have a high conflict divorce or custody case.

Goal-directed treatment planning aims at providing stabilization of the immediate and most problematic presenting issues at the beginning of treatment with an ability to allow the treatment plan to evolve as needed (Nurcombe, 1989). By first identifying the presenting problems, it very simple to establish the goals of therapy. Creating objectives that can be measurable is simply a matter of asking yourself, *"How will I know that we are making progress toward the goal?"* Establishing measures for progress in the form of objectives helps you, the parents, the child client and the court focus on the purpose and process of the therapy. It is advisable that for each goal you have at least two objectives and at least two interventions to work toward meeting those objectives. An example:

Presenting problem: *Child client is having nightmares and inability to sleep independently due to high levels of anxiety at night ever since father moved out of the house.*

Working diagnosis: *Adjustment Disorder*

Goal #1: *Child will sleep in his own bed while managing anxious feelings independently.*

Objective #1: *Child will remain in his own bed at least one night in a week by the end of the month and at least 2 nights by the middle of next month as reported by the mother.*

Objective #2: *Child will develop, practice and utilize self-soothing skills before and during bedtime as reported by child and mother using the self-soothing skills chart.*

Interventions:

1. Child-centered play therapy in session based on meta-analytic research showing significant outcomes with children experiencing anxiety.

2. Bibliotherapy and Workbook (*What to Do When You Dread Your Bed*) with CBT skill-building implementation.

3. Parent-child dyadic sessions with each parent to assess and address attachments and enhance healthy bonding.

Record Keeping

It is always possible that any of your clinical records could be subpoenaed, so it's important to follow these guidelines for all your cases. For high conflict divorce and custody cases, it's all the more important to cross all the T's and dot all the I's. Here are some specific guidelines to consider:

1. Record all background, presenting problems and symptoms, present context, history and reports of both parents from the intakes, thoroughly leaving out any premature conceptualization.

2. Be sure to file any and all emails, texts or other written correspondence received from both parents, lawyers and guardian ad litem.

3. Every time you have a phone conversation with either parent, the child's teachers, a lawyer, other mental health professionals involved or the guardian ad litem, document the conversation in the file, noting the start and end time for the conversation, the topic of the conversation and any notable things said by you or the other party.

4. Utilize an electronic health record system so your notes will all be uniform and will include all of the important components of a clinical record in one place including

records of payment, diagnosis, progress, prognosis, dates and times of sessions, treatment plan, intake notes, your session notes and all other correspondence and notes of all other communications.

5. Keep your session notes clean, clinical, thorough, without unnecessary commentary. Report what interventions were utilized and the degree to which the client partici-pated, along with any observations of notable themes in the child's play and any significant self-report from the child. If you are providing child-centered play therapy, be sure to make consistent notation of your use of track-ing, reflection, therapeutic limit setting and examples of returning responsibility to the child. Document the toys the child chooses, the apparent mood and affect of the child and any structure or direction you may have included. Make notes as to who brought the child to session, who else may have accompanied the child to your office, if the parent was on time and any significant conversation or events before or after the session with the parent(s) or siblings as it may be relevant to the child's progress or lack thereof. Report factual observations. Any concerns or conceptualizing thoughts recorded in the record should be framed in clean and clinical language steering clear of any emotion or reactivity in your notes. Be cautious not to form sweeping opinions of any kind in your notes.

6. Maintain the completion of your notes in a timely fashion so that if asked on the stand about this you can confi-dently testify that you always complete session notes the same day as the session or right after sessions to ensure your observations and memories of such are clearly and accurately recorded.

7. Anything you write in the record could potentially be scrutinized and even released into the public as evidence in a court case. You will, of course, take every measure to ethically protect the record and therefore the wellbeing of your client, but in the case you are forced to allow your record to be seen by the parents, the guardian ad litem, lawyers and the court, be mindful of how you word and record your clinical observations and recommendations.

8. When writing parenting recommendations and recording session notes after parent sessions, utilize the bill of rights as the framework for your recommendations that you give to all parents who are divorced or divorcing. Make the same recommendations to both parents in one letter or email so that neither parent feels singled out and so that you cannot be accused of bias.

9. You might consider using a coding system for observations in session that would make it more appealing for a party to receive a summary of treatment in place of the actual record. Always encourage parties to allow you to prepare a summary of treatment rather than the actual clinical record. In a summary you can more easily enumerate the basic facts of the course of treatment in case there are phrases in the record you'd prefer the parties not pick apart in court.

10. Update the treatment plan as needed, and document that you have provided all versions of the treatment plan to the parents and offered opportunity to meet in parent sessions to review the treatment plan and the progress of therapy, including measuring the specific progress toward established objectives.

CHAPTER 10

Preparing for Going to Court

I PREFER TO HELP therapists preserve the integrity of the therapeutic relationship by taking measures to avoid having to testify in court. The reality is that all of those efforts do not prevent the fact that therapists are frequently subpoenaed to court in high conflict divorce and custody cases. It is, therefore, best to be prepared.

What to do with a subpoena?

If you've never been served with a subpoena, I'll tell you the first time can be a bit unnerving. Understanding how it works and what to do in advance can help you feel more confident. A subpoena is a legal document prepared according to your state's civil or criminal practice rules and your state's supreme court rules that dictates you must appear in court for a particular case that is coming before a judge. Subpoenas are typically requested by an attorney who wishes to have you serve as a witness in the case being presented in court, issued by the court clerk, and then usually served (delivered in a particular manner) by someone called a *process server* or sometimes by a sheriff or sheriff's deputy.

There are generally two kinds of subpoena, and it is common for therapists to receive one or both:

Subpoena ad testificandum: This type of subpoena requires you to appear and provide testimony to a court or other legal authority. You have the legal right to have an attorney represent you when you appear.

Subpoena duces tecum: This type of subpoena will require you to provide evidence usually in the form of your clinical notes and record.

Below are some suggested guidelines on what to do when you receive a subpoena based upon guidance I myself have received from my own legal counsel over the years. Keep in mind, laws regarding subpoenas and legal proceedings may differ from state to state. (*Please invest in hiring your own legal counsel or call your own liability insurance to receive appropriate legal guidance of your own*):

1. Do not ignore a subpoena. A subpoena is a court ordered, mandated call for you to appear and/or produce particular evidence. You must respond appropriately.

2. Contact your liability insurance carrier immediately. File an office report with your carrier and request a legal consultation. If your carrier and coverage does not include legal consultation, contact a local attorney who is familiar with health care law to review the subpoena and advise you.

3. Contact both parents of your child client, and inform them that you have received a subpoena and request they sign a release and waiver for you to testify and/or speak with the attorney issuing the subpoena if needed. Be sure

to inform your own attorney of whether the clients have provided release and waiver.

Paying for legal consultation and representation is simply a cost of doing business as a mental health professional. Some liability insurance companies are generous with this as a service you are paying for and others are not. It's wise when shopping for liability insurance that you seek a plan that offers legal consultation when you are served with a subpoena along with other related legal matters that arise. Otherwise, you may have to pay out of pocket attorney's fees for necessary legal consultation. It is not wise to try to handle legal matters without your own legal advice and representation.

There are certain circumstances when a subpoena may be *quashed* or you may be released, but I defer to your own attorney or liability insurance carrier to advise you on those procedures.

Preparing for Court Testimony

Your own legal counsel will advise you on what to do if either of the legal clients (parents) have refused to provide release and waiver of confidentiality for the purposes of testimony, as this creates an ethical and legal dilemma for you. I strongly recommend you obtain legal advice on this topic. Failing this, if you are unclear, you may request the judge provide you direction before the questioning begins citing your state's statute providing client privilege and HIPAA laws. Typically, a judge has the authority to overrule those laws and require you to testify if they so choose, but it may differ state to state so please consult your own legal counsel.

Otherwise, below is some general guidance on how to be best prepared for testifying in court. Review this with your own attorney and defer to his/her guidance if it differs from what I am sharing with you here:

1. If your clinical record has been subpoenaed, ask your own attorney if there is a way for you to prepare a summary of treatment in lieu of taking your record to court. If your attorney is unable to confirm this is sufficient and your clinical record has specifically been subpoenaed, take a copy of your record, not the actual record itself, with you to court. Prepare a summary of treatment for your own use. This will allow you to have a quick look at dates and highlights from the clinical record when you are being questioned.

2. Be well prepared to name and describe your professional credentials and area of expertise. Update and review your curriculum vitae (CV or resume) and be able to answer any questions about your professional capabilities and expertise. Bring your CV and your summary of treatment

3. Dress appropriately for court. No need for a power suit, but dress pants, a blazer or professional cardigan, close-toed dress shoes, solid colors, and refrain from bright or flashy jewelry or makeup.

4. Arrive at the courthouse thirty minutes early so you can locate the courtroom and review your notes before the proceedings begin.

5. Sit, walk and stand tall. Upright posture commands respect.

6. If the judge addresses you, you will respond by addressing the judge as "Your Honor."

Court is a polite place and you will need to remain polite no matter what is asked of you and no matter how an attorney may attempt to rattle you or question your integrity or professionalism on the stand. Keep in mind, it is not uncommon for one side to attempt to discredit your authority if your testimony may be harmful to their case. Once you are sworn in as a witness, you will likely be qualified as an *expert witness,* which renders you the ability to provide opinion. You will be asked questions about your education, credentials and experience. If not, you are simply a *fact witness* and can only answer questions with a matter of actual fact without opinion included.

- When you are asked questions, answer the questions with short and direct answers. Do not read into the question. Do not provide explanations or opinions unless the court instructs you to. Allow the attorneys to do their job of stringing together questions that will draw information from you as needed.

- You may ask for a question to be repeated or clarified if you are unclear as to what is being asked of you.

- Take your time. Remember your role. Think about your answer before answering. Be sure you are prepared to state what your role is and what your role is not if you are asked questions that sound like they are asking for your opinion on custody issues.

- Speak slowly and directly into the microphone so that the court reporter is able to record your answers easily and accurately.

It's important to block off as much of your day as possible when you are required to go to court because you simply can't easily predict how long the wait may be before you are called into the courtroom to testify or how long you will be on the stand. It's also best to have your mind focused fully on the case at hand; so, refrain from multi-tasking or scheduling other clients for that day if you can.

CHAPTER 11

Attending to Your Self-Care

Self-care is an Ethical Issue

Τ HE 2014 *ACA Code of Ethics* includes the statement that "Counselors engage in self-care activities to maintain and promote their own emotional, physical, mental and spiritual wellbeing to best meet their professional responsibilities." While the NASW ethics code does not specifically state self care is an ethical issue, it is clearly implied by emphasis in one section on a social worker's obligation to address a colleague's failure to attend to self-care that could be of resulting harm to a client. The AAMFT ethical code is clear that therapists must address any impairment in their ability to provide client services by seeking professional support.

The ACA Code of Ethics (2014), in section C.2.g., implicitly states that:

Counselors monitor themselves for signs of impairment from their own physical, mental or emotional problems and refrain from offering or providing professional services when impaired. They seek assistance for problems that reach the level of professional impairment, and, if necessary, they limit, suspend or terminate their professional responsibilities until it is determined that they may safely resume their work. (p. 9)

We need to focus on our personal vulnerabilities before they lead us to unethical professional behavior. Knowing our own vulnerabilities enables us to employ the methods and means to ensuring our personal needs are so well cared for that those needs do not show up within the therapy process and do harm to the client and the therapeutic relationship. Therapists must understand their own personal pieces and parts that are still in need of attention and healing.

"Some healthcare providers who have been punished by their licensing board, hospital board, or practice group for an ethics violation tell similar stories of being under unusual levels of stress because of a family member who was ill. In that context, they deviated from their usual behavior." – Claire Zilber, MD.

It is all too common for healthcare professionals to underestimate the effects of stress on professional behavior with clients. Proactive measures and greater awareness to the effects of stress proactively can be an important means of mitigating such risk. It is important to remember that balance is especially important given our unique occupational vulnerabilities, enabling us to be more present and effective with our clients, and encourages more rewards in all aspects of our lives. Balance is not necessarily a fixed destination, rather it is a constant process. If you decide to stand on one leg, eventually you will find yourself wobbling a bit to the right and a bit to the left, but this wobbling is also part of the process of finding balance. Once we find it, we surely will fall off balance, so engaging in purposeful activities that help us to not fall too far off balance is key.

In order to cope, therapists absolutely need inner strength, resilience, hope, sources of encouragement, self-soothing skills and awareness of our own strengths as well as our own vulnerabilities. In order to do the work of psychotherapy with families going through high conflict divorce and custody disputes, we have to know these cases come with potential hazards. We have a whole other job to do in order to ensure those hazards do not impair our ability to provide quality therapy services for our clients. That other job we have to do is to ensure we have a plan for self-care.

Even when we are well aware of the damages we've suffered in the distant or recent past, we are at risk of falling into a dangerous trap of inadvertently projecting all of our own personal wounds onto our clients, so it is essential to uphold our ethical principles and commit to conscious and active attention to self-care as a matter of ethical obligation.

Deep and broad self-knowledge and self-awareness is crucial for helping to prevent this above-mentioned trap. But it's also critically important to seek support. This support might be through supervision, consultation, your own psychotherapy, professional groups and other professional networks in order to purposefully create and seek social support from friends. It's important to develop an arsenal of healthy coping methods like mindfulness meditation, journaling, exercising, cultivating a healthy sense of humor and keeping a positive, hopeful attitude.

Be aware that working with families embroiled in high conflict battles can quickly take its toll on you. It is clinically and ethically necessary that you implement a firm set of policies and protocols for limiting your contact with the parents of your child clients with clear structure so that their warring does not spill over onto you and your own life.

Rather than only focusing on self-care techniques, Norcross (2000) recommends developing specific strategies in order to ensure self-awareness and self-care are implemented effectively. You need a dedicated plan for daily, weekly, monthly, and annual self-care.

Here is an exercise I have used to help therapists create their self-care plan in my mentoring, supervision and retreats for therapists:

An Exercise for Developing Your Self-Care Plan

1. Take a piece of paper and draw a line horizontally across the middle of the page.

2. In the bottom half divide into 3 equal size columns with vertical lines.

3. In the top half divide into 2 equal size columns with vertical lines.

4. Label the top two columns in this order: Daily, Weekly.

5. Label the bottom three columns in this order: Monthly, Quarterly, Annually.

6. In the Daily section write down all of the things you will plan to do for your self care on a daily basis. Then review, and if it seems unrealistic, maybe move some of those to your weekly column. (i.e. Daily = floss teeth, meditate, drink ½ gallon of water; Weekly = go to yoga class; go to church, call my mom)

7. Add the activities you will do for yourself in the monthly, quarterly and annual columns (i.e Monthly = get massage, preview budget, have game night with friends; Quarterly = clean out clothing closet, attend a concert, have a health check-up; Annually = go on retreat, take a week-long vacation).

8. Transfer all of these items onto your calendar. Review and observe these commitments as your plan for caring for yourself.

Having a plan that is plugged into your calendar for your own self-care will help you to maintain your own wellbeing and will help you to provide the best services for your clients as a result.

CHAPTER 12

Conclusion

Providing psychotherapy services for children and families who are experiencing high conflict in matters of divorce and custody dispute can be some of the most challenging cases you will have in your career. Most mental health graduate programs do not prepare for students for the complexities of these kinds of cases and all too often therapists unwittingly find themselves in the middle of the intractable dynamics of parents at war. It can be a very disorienting and anxiety provoking set of circumstances and often the typical ways of managing a case does not work and my make matters worse.

Having methods for careful screening, gathering as much information in the beginning and setting clear and firm boundaries from the start will help you to avoid stepping on landmines or falling into unforeseen court-involved matters. I believe a lot of therapists are in such a rush to fill their caseload in private practice that they go full steam ahead and miss the yellow and red flags. Taking the time to do the careful screening on the front end will help you to be sure the clients you are accepting are the right clients for you and your practice.

In cases where therapists are employed by an agency or contracted in a group practice it may not always be possible to do that initial phone call screening or conduct the intake session as I am suggesting. You may have to find a creative way to participate in the process of screening potential clients before you see them for therapy services. It might be wise to share this book with your agency or practice director and start a discussion about ways the organization might improve the screening process to ensure best fit for potential clients and therapists.

I hear therapists bemoan not having money to hire an attorney. I don't think you can afford to not hire an attorney if you're going to be accepting high conflict cases. Seeking sound legal guidance proactively is an investment worth making. Find a liability insurance carrier that will provide legal consultation when needed. If you have to pay more for a better service, then do so. If you're in private practice, I urge you to consider paying for legal consultation to be an important cost of doing business.

Don't go it alone. You can and should seek private case consultation and supervision regardless of how long you've been licensed and practicing. Invest in a mentor. Pay for consultation. Go to supervision throughout your career. With these kinds of cases it will be essential. You might create a peer consultation group with other therapists who have read this book and work with these cases so that you can all support one another. There are many ways to ensure you have connection so that you don't end up feeling isolated and anxious without support.

Keep your eyes and ears open wide. Listen. Gather information before agreeing to take on the case. Don't jump to conclusions. Inquire until you have a full and clear picture. Watch for the yellow and red flags. Get your policies and protocols in order and be sure you are enforcing and following those policies and protocols. With preparation and a well-organized plan for treatment and for your own self-care, you can be confident that you have covered your bases.

About the Author

 **Lynn Louise Wonders, LPC, RPT-S, CPCS** is a Registered Play Therapist-Supervisor, licensed and certified in the state of Georgia to provide professional counseling and supervision services. She is the Director of Wonders Counseling & Consulting Services based in metro Atlanta, Georgia, providing consultation and mentoring services for therapists throughout the United States, Israel, Ireland, England, Australia and South Korea. Ms. Wonders is the founder of the Preschool Emotion Education Program (PEEP) implemented in preschool settings since 2003 to provide young children, teachers and parents with experiential education and support to facilitate mindfulness and emotional intelligence. She is the founder of Parenting with Purpose and Vision Seminar Series and is a trained facilitator of Drs. John & Julie Gottman's methods of couples counseling and parenting training programs. Ms. Wonders is an Association for Play Therapy Approved Provider and has been providing play therapy training and continuing education for therapists in person and online since 2011. She is the Early Childhood Specialist and National Spokesperson for Primrose Schools having authored numerous published articles on subjects of early childhood development and parenting. She

has served as a guest instructor for the psychology department at Berry College in Rome, Georgia and for the mental health departments at Grady Hospital, Peachford Hospital and Mercy Care Center in Atlanta. Ms. Wonders is also the Director for Wonders Wellness Institute for Women through which she offers self-care retreats and provides consultation, resources and education on the subject of sustaining a healthy holistic lifestyle. She has well over 20 years of experience teaching meditation, mindfulness and gentle forms of yoga and Tai Chi & Chi Kung. Ms. Wonders has led self-care retreats for women in the North Georgia mountains since 2011. You can learn more about her services at www.WondersCounseling.com and www.WondersWellness.com

References

Amato. P., Loomis, L., & Booth, A. (1995). Parental divorce, parental marital conflict, and offspring well-being during early adulthood. *Social Forces, 73,* 895-916.

Buchanan, C., Maccoby, E., & Dornbusch, S.(1991). Caught between parents: Adolescents' experience in divorced homes. *Child Development,* 62, 1008-1029.

Buehler, C., Krishnakumar, A., Stone, *G.,* Anthony, C., Pemberton, S., Gerard, J., & Barber, B. K. (1998). Interparental conflict styles and youth problem behaviors: A two-sample replication study. *Journal of Marriage & Family, 60,* 119-132.

Corey, G. (2018). *Counselor self-care.* Alexandria, VA: American Counseling Association.

Cornell Law School Staff. (2018). Guardian Ad Litem. Retrieved from https://www.law.cornell.edu/wex/guardian_ad_litem

Cummings. E., & Davies, P. (1994). *Children and marital conflict.* New York: Guilford.

Diagnosis. (2018). Retrieved from https://www.dictionary.com/browse/diagnosis

Gardner, R. A. (1998). *The Parental Alienation Syndrome* (2nd ed.). Creskill, NJ: Creative Therapeutics.

Gardner, R. A. (2002). Parental Alienation Syndrome vs. Parental Alienation: Which Diagnosis Should Evaluators Use in Child-Custody Disputes? *The American Journal of Family Therapy,30*(2), 93-115. doi:10.1080/019261802753573821

Grych. J., & Fincham,F.(1993).Children's appraisal of marital conflict: Initial investigations of the cognitive-contextual framework.*Child Development,*64.215-230.

Guillen, L. (2013, January 03). Children's Bill of Rights in Divorce. Retrieved from https://www.divorcenet.com/states/texas/txart32

Halikias, W. (2005). The Guardian Ad Litem For Children In Divorce. *Family Court Review,32*(4), 490-501.

Health Insurance Portability and Accountability Act of 1996. (2016, October 10). Retrieved from https://aspe.hhs.gov/report/health-insurance-portability-and-accountability-act-1996

Johnston, J. R. (1994). High-Conflict Divorce. *The Future of Children,4*(1), 165.

Johnston, J. R. (2005). Research Update. *Family Court Review,33*(4), 415-425.

Johnston, J., & Roseby, V. (2005). In the Name of the Child: A Developmental Approach to Understanding and Helping Children of Conflicted and Violent Divorce. *Family Court Review,36*(2), 317-319. doi:10.1111/j.174-1617.1998.tb00511.x

Kelly, J. B. (2000). Children's adjustment in conflicted marriage and divorce: A decade review of research. *Journal* of *American Academy of Child and Adolescent Psychiatry,* 39(8), 963-973

Kline, M., Johnston, J., & Tschann, J. (1990). The long shadow of marital conflict: A model of children's post divorce adjustment. *Journal of Marriage & Family,* 53,297-309.

Kelly, J. B., & Johnston, J. R. (2001). The alienated child: A reformulation of parental alienation syndrome. *Family Court Review,* 39(3), 249-266.

Lorandos D, Bernet W, & Sauber RS, eds. *Parental Alienation: The Handbook for Mental Health and Legal Professionals.* Springfield, IL: Charles C Thomas Publisher; 2013

Marshack, K. (2000). Recognizing high conflict divorce. Retrieved from http://www.kmarshack.com/High-Conflict-Divorce/Recognizing-High-Conflict-Divorce.html

Mullen, J. A., & Rickli, J. M. (2014). *Child-centered play therapy workbook: A self-directed guide for professionals.* Champaign, IL: Research Press.

Norcross, J. C. (2000). Psychotherapist self-care: Practitioner-tested, research-informed strategies. *Professional Psychology: Research and Practice, 31*(6), 710-713.

Nurcombe B. (1989(Goal-directed treatment planning and the principles of brief hospitalization. *Journal of American Academy of Child & Adolescent Psychiatry.* (1):26-30. PubMed, PMID: 2914832.

Potegal, M., Carlson, G. A., Margulies, D., Basile, J., Gutkovich, Z. A., & Wall, M. (2009). The behavioral organization, temporal characteristics, and diagnostic concomitants of rage outbursts in child psychiatric inpatients. *Current psychiatry reports, 11*(2), 127-33.

The Alienated Child. (n.d.). *Conducting Child Custody Evaluations: From Basic to Complex Issues,*183-204.

Vandewater, E.,& Lansford, J.(1998).Influences of family structure and parental conflict on children's well-being. *Family Relations,* 47, 323-330.

Walters, M. G., & Friedlander, S. (2016). When a Child Rejects a Parent: Working With the Intractable Resist/Refuse Dynamic. *Family Court Review,54*(3), 424-445.

Additional Resources

Lynn Louise Wonders is available for professional consultation with therapists and can be reached through her website at www. WondersCounseling.com

There are recorded trainings available for continuing education under approved providers for NBCC and APT for therapists also available at www.WondersCounseling.com

For information about collaborative family law please visit https://www.collaborativepractice.com

Made in the USA
Columbia, SC
26 January 2020

87158719R00065